Credit Forge

A Blueprint to Building Business Credit

Antwone Dixon

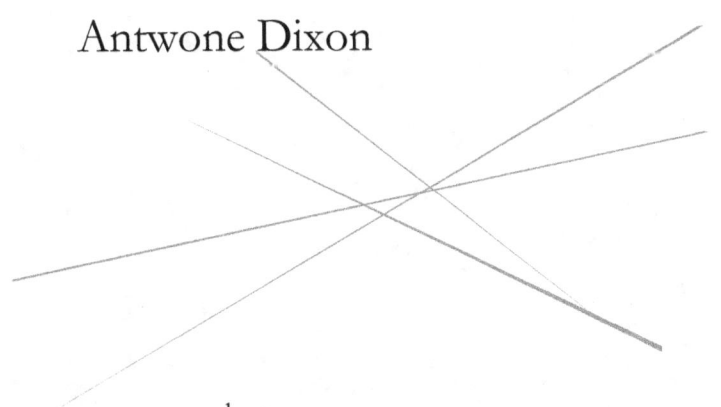

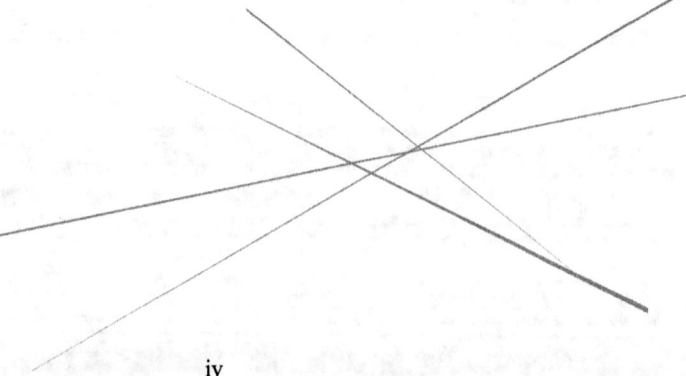

DEDICATION

This book is dedicated to all the aspiring entrepreneurs and small business owners who dare to dream big and strive for success. May you find inspiration, guidance, and empowerment within these pages as you embark on your journey to master the art of business credit. Your dedication, resilience, and passion are the driving forces behind innovation and progress, and it is with great admiration and respect that I dedicate this book to you. May your entrepreneurial spirit continue to flourish, and may you achieve all your aspirations and goals.

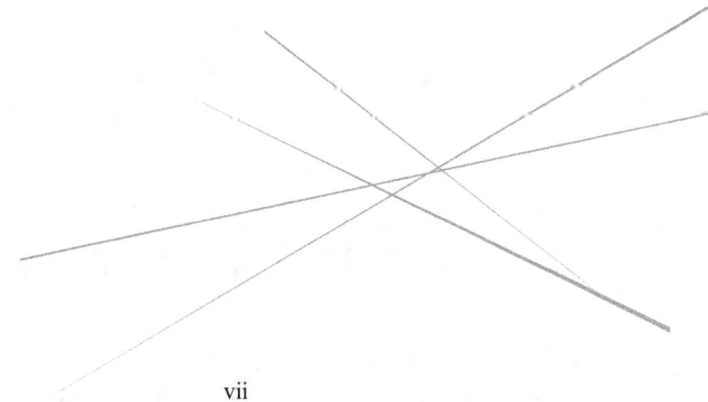

CONTENTS

ACKNOWLEDGMENTS

I would like to express my deepest gratitude to my wife, whose unwavering support and understanding have been the cornerstone of my journey. Her encouragement, patience, and belief in me have fueled my determination to succeed and overcome challenges along the way. I am also grateful for the wisdom and guidance of the "old man" who has been a source of inspiration and mentorship throughout my career. His invaluable advice, experience, and encouragement have shaped my perspective and contributed to my growth as a business professional. To my wife and the old man, thank you for your love, support, and belief in me. Your contributions have been instrumental in my success, and I am forever grateful for your presence in my life.

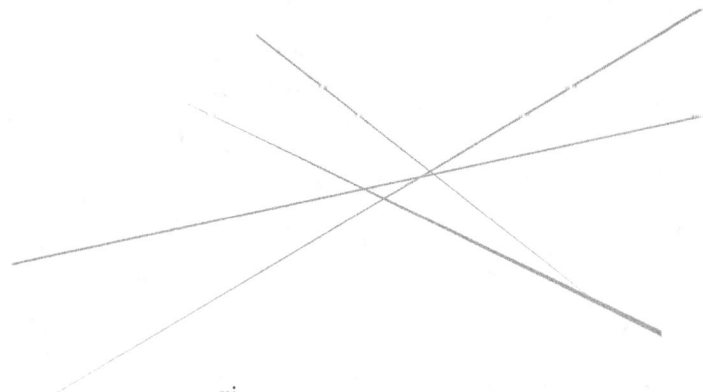

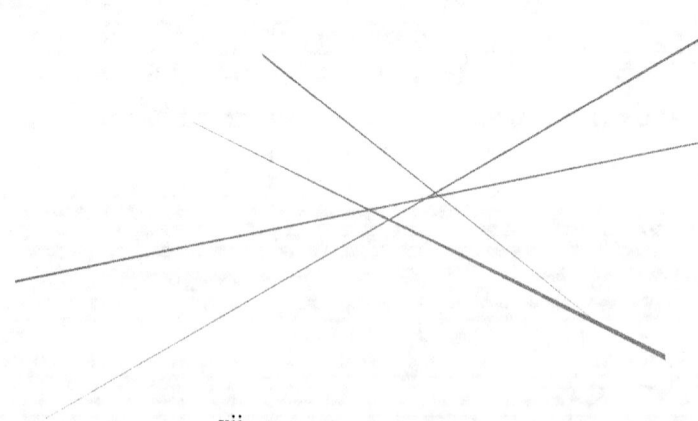

CHAPTER 1: UNDERSTANDING BUSINESS CREDIT

Welcome to Chapter 1 of "Credit Forge: A Blueprint for Business Credit Building." In this chapter, we will delve into the fundamentals of business credit and its importance for entrepreneurs and small business owners. Understanding business credit is essential for navigating the financial landscape effectively and building a strong foundation for long-term success.

1.1 Definition and Significance:

Business credit refers to the creditworthiness of a business entity, separate from its owners or operators. It encompasses the business's ability to borrow money, obtain goods or services on credit terms, and establish financial relationships with creditors and suppliers. Establishing and maintaining good business credit is crucial for accessing financing, negotiating favorable terms, and building trust with stakeholders.

1.2 Distinction Between Personal and Business Credit:

It's important to differentiate between personal and business credit to avoid commingling finances and protect personal assets. While personal credit is tied to an individual's financial history, business credit assesses the creditworthiness of a business entity. Understanding this distinction helps entrepreneurs manage finances effectively, establish legal separation, and access financing based on their business's merits.

1.3 The Impact of Business Credit on Growth:

Business credit plays a pivotal role in facilitating business growth and expansion. A strong credit profile enables businesses to access capital, negotiate favorable terms with vendors and suppliers, and seize growth opportunities. By establishing good business credit, entrepreneurs can fuel innovation, invest in strategic initiatives, and position their businesses for long-term success in competitive markets.

1.4 Establishing Objectives:

As entrepreneurs embark on their business credit-building journey, it's crucial to set clear objectives aligned with their business goals. Whether it's securing financing for expansion, improving cash flow management, or enhancing vendor relationships, defining specific objectives helps guide credit-building efforts and measure progress over time.

1.5 Assessing Current Knowledge:

Before diving deeper into business credit, it's beneficial for entrepreneurs to assess their current understanding and knowledge gaps. By evaluating their familiarity with credit concepts, credit reporting agencies, and credit-building strategies, entrepreneurs can identify areas for improvement and tailor their learning experience to meet their needs effectively.

Conclusion: In conclusion, Chapter 1 has provided an overview of business credit and its significance for entrepreneurs and small business owners. Understanding the fundamentals of business credit is essential for navigating the financial landscape, accessing financing, and fostering long-term growth and success. As we proceed further in this book, we will explore strategies for building and managing business credit effectively to achieve your business objectives

CHAPTER 2: THE BASICS OF BUSINESS CREDIT

Welcome to Chapter 2 of "Credit Forge: A Blueprint for Business Credit Building." In this chapter, we will explore the foundational elements of business credit and why it's essential for entrepreneurs and small business owners to understand. By grasping the basics of business credit, you'll be better equipped to navigate the complexities of credit-building and financial management for your business.

2.1 Understanding Business Credit:

Business credit is the assessment of a business entity's creditworthiness based on its financial history, payment behavior, and overall financial health. Unlike personal credit, which pertains to individuals, business credit focuses on the creditworthiness of the business itself, separate from its owners or operators. This distinction is crucial for establishing legal separation, protecting personal assets, and accessing financing based on the business's merits.

2.2 Importance of Business Credit:

The significance of business credit cannot be overstated for entrepreneurs and small business owners. It serves as a critical tool for accessing financing, negotiating favorable terms with suppliers

4

and vendors, and building trust and credibility with stakeholders. A strong business credit profile opens doors to growth opportunities, enhances financial stability, and strengthens the overall viability of the business in the marketplace.

2.3 Components of Business Credit:

Business credit is influenced by various factors, including payment history, credit utilization, length of credit history, public records, and industry risk. These components collectively shape a business's credit profile and determine its creditworthiness in the eyes of lenders, suppliers, and other creditors. Understanding the key components of business credit empowers entrepreneurs to proactively manage their credit and maximize their borrowing potential.

2.4 Establishing Business Credit:

Building a solid business credit profile requires proactive steps, including obtaining a separate Employer Identification Number (EIN), opening a dedicated business bank account, and establishing trade lines with vendors and suppliers who report to credit bureaus. By taking these initial steps and making timely payments, businesses can lay the foundation for a strong credit history and improve their creditworthiness over time.

2.5 Benefits of Good Business Credit:

Good business credit offers a myriad of benefits, including easier access to financing, lower interest rates on loans and credit cards, enhanced negotiating power with suppliers, and improved cash flow management. By maintaining a positive credit profile, businesses can position themselves for long-term success, growth, and resilience in the face of economic challenges.

Conclusion:

In conclusion, Chapter 2 has provided an overview of the basics of business credit and its importance for entrepreneurs and small business owners. By understanding the fundamentals of business credit, you'll be better equipped to navigate the credit-building process, access financing, and unlock opportunities for growth and success in your business endeavors. As we delve deeper into this book, we'll explore strategies for effectively building, managing, and leveraging business credit to achieve your business goals.

CHAPTER 3: YOUR BUSINESS CREDIT

Welcome to Chapter 3 of "Credit Forge: A Blueprint for Business Credit Building." In this chapter, we will delve into the specific steps you can take to establish and manage your business credit effectively. Understanding how to navigate the intricacies of your business credit is essential for entrepreneurs and small business owners looking to access financing, negotiate favorable terms, and build a strong financial foundation for their businesses.

3.1 Obtaining Your Business Identification:

The first step in establishing your business credit is obtaining a separate Employer Identification Number (EIN) from the Internal Revenue Service (IRS). This unique identifier distinguishes your business from your personal finances and is essential for opening business bank accounts, applying for credit, and filing taxes as a business entity.

3.2 Establishing a Dedicated Business Bank Account:

Opening a dedicated business bank account is crucial for managing your business finances separately from your personal finances. This account should be used exclusively for business transactions, including receiving payments, paying expenses, and building a positive financial history that contributes to your business credit profile.

3.3 Building Initial Trade Lines:

Building trade lines with vendors and suppliers who report to credit bureaus is an effective way to establish your business credit. Look for suppliers willing to extend credit terms and make timely payments to demonstrate your business's creditworthiness. Consistently meeting payment obligations will help build a positive payment history and strengthen your business credit profile over time.

3.4 Leveraging Business Credit Cards:

Applying for a business credit card is another strategy for building and managing your business credit. Choose a card that offers favorable terms and rewards that align with your business needs. Use the card responsibly, making timely payments and keeping balances low relative to your credit limit, to demonstrate financial responsibility and improve your creditworthiness.

3.5 Monitoring Your Business Credit:

Regularly monitoring your business credit report from major credit bureaus, such as Dun & Bradstreet, Experian, and Equifax, is essential for staying informed about your credit standing. Check your credit report for inaccuracies or errors and dispute any discrepancies promptly. Monitoring your credit also allows you to track your progress and identify areas for improvement in your credit profile.

Conclusion:

In conclusion, Chapter 3 has provided actionable steps for establishing and managing your business credit effectively. By obtaining a separate business identification, opening a dedicated business bank account, building trade lines with vendors, leveraging business credit cards, and monitoring your credit report, you can lay the foundation for a strong business credit profile. As you continue your credit-building journey, remember to prioritize financial responsibility, timely payments, and proactive credit management to achieve long-term success and growth in your business

CHAPTER 4: CREDIT MANAGEMENT STRATEGIES

Welcome to Chapter 4 of "Credit Forge: A Blueprint for Business Credit Building." In this chapter, we will explore effective credit management strategies that entrepreneurs and small business owners can implement to optimize their business credit profiles. By understanding and applying these strategies, you can proactively manage your credit, mitigate risks, and maximize your borrowing potential.

4.1 Establishing Credit Policies and Procedures:

Developing clear credit policies and procedures is essential for managing credit effectively. Define credit terms, payment schedules, and credit limits for customers and clients. Establish protocols for credit applications, credit checks, and collections to ensure consistency and compliance with credit policies.

4.2 Monitoring Credit Utilization:

Monitoring your credit utilization ratio—the percentage of available credit you're using—can help you manage your credit effectively. Aim to keep your credit utilization ratio below 30% to demonstrate responsible credit usage and avoid overextending your credit. Regularly review your credit card balances and credit limits to stay within your target utilization range.

4.3 Timely Payments:

Making timely payments on your credit accounts is crucial for maintaining a positive credit history and improving your credit score. Set up automatic payments or reminders to ensure you pay your bills on time, every time. Late payments can negatively impact your credit score and erode trust with creditors, so prioritize timely payments to preserve your creditworthiness.

4.4 Managing Debt Wisely:

Managing debt wisely involves balancing your business's borrowing needs with its ability to repay debt responsibly. Avoid taking on excessive debt that exceeds your business's cash flow and revenue capacity. Focus on paying down high-interest debt first and consider consolidating or refinancing debt to lower interest rates and improve cash flow management.

4.5 Diversifying Credit Sources:

Diversifying your credit sources can help you build a robust credit profile and reduce reliance on any single creditor or credit product. Consider establishing trade lines with multiple vendors and suppliers, applying for business credit cards from different issuers, and exploring various financing options, such as loans, lines of credit, and leases.

4.6 Monitoring and Reviewing Credit Reports:

Regularly monitoring your business credit reports from major credit bureaus allows you to stay informed about your credit standing and detect any errors or inaccuracies that may impact your creditworthiness. Review your credit reports at least annually and dispute any discrepancies promptly to ensure the accuracy of your credit information.

Conclusion:

In conclusion, Chapter 4 has provided valuable insights into credit management strategies for entrepreneurs and small business owners. By establishing credit policies and procedures, monitoring credit utilization, making timely payments, managing debt wisely, diversifying credit sources, and monitoring and reviewing credit reports, you can effectively manage your business credit and position your business for long-term success and growth. As you implement these strategies, remember to prioritize financial responsibility, proactive credit management, and continuous improvement to achieve your credit-building goals.

CHAPTER 5: ACCESSING FINANCING OPTIONS

Welcome to Chapter 5 of "Credit Forge: A Blueprint for Business Credit Building." In this chapter, we will explore various financing options available to entrepreneurs and small business owners. Whether you're looking to fund startup costs, expand operations, or manage cash flow, understanding these financing options can help you make informed decisions and access the capital your business needs to thrive.

5.1 Traditional Bank Loans:

Traditional bank loans are a common financing option for businesses with established credit and a strong financial track record. These loans typically offer competitive interest rates and repayment terms but may require collateral and a lengthy application process. Prepare a comprehensive business plan, financial statements, and documentation to support your loan application and increase your chances of approval.

5.2 Small Business Administration (SBA) Loans:

SBA loans are guaranteed by the U.S. Small Business Administration and are designed to support small businesses with financing needs. These loans offer favorable terms and lower down payments compared to traditional bank loans, making them an attractive option for startups and small businesses. Explore SBA loan programs, such as 7(a) loans, CDC/504 loans, and microloans, to find the best fit for your business needs.

5.3 Business Lines of Credit:

A business line of credit provides businesses with flexible access to funds for short-term financing needs, such as managing cash flow fluctuations, covering operating expenses, or seizing growth opportunities. Unlike traditional term loans, lines of credit allow you to borrow funds as needed, up to a predetermined credit limit, and repay only the amount borrowed plus interest.

5.4 Business Credit Cards:

Business credit cards offer a convenient and flexible financing option for businesses to cover day-to-day expenses, make purchases, and manage cash flow. These cards typically come with rewards programs, expense tracking tools, and benefits tailored to business needs. Compare different business credit card options, consider factors like interest rates, rewards, and fees, and choose the card that best aligns with your business goals.

5.5 Alternative Financing Solutions:

In addition to traditional financing options, entrepreneurs can explore alternative financing solutions to meet their business's unique needs. These may include invoice financing, merchant cash advances, equipment financing, peer-to-peer lending, crowdfunding, and angel or venture capital funding. Evaluate the pros and cons of each alternative financing option and choose the one that best suits your business's financial situation and growth objectives.

5.6 Building Relationships with Lenders and Investors:

Building relationships with lenders, investors, and financial institutions is essential for accessing financing options and securing favorable terms. Network with local banks, credit unions, community development financial institutions (CDFIs), and venture capital firms. Attend networking events, pitch competitions, and industry conferences to connect with potential lenders and investors and showcase your business's value proposition and growth potential.

Conclusion:

In conclusion, Chapter 5 has provided an overview of various financing options available to entrepreneurs and small business owners. By exploring traditional bank loans, SBA loans, business lines of credit, business credit cards, alternative financing solutions, and building relationships with lenders and investors, you can access the capital your business needs to succeed and grow. As you evaluate financing options, consider factors like interest rates, repayment terms, eligibility requirements, and potential impact on your business's financial health and long-term objectives. With careful planning and strategic decision-making, you can find the right financing solution to support your business's growth and success.

CHAPTER 6: BUILDING STRONG CREDIT PROFILES

Welcome to Chapter 6 of "Credit Forge: A Blueprint for Business Credit Building." In this chapter, we will explore strategies for building strong credit profiles for your business. A robust credit profile is essential for accessing financing, negotiating favorable terms, and building trust with creditors and suppliers. By implementing these strategies, you can establish a solid foundation for your business's creditworthiness and financial success.

6.1 Establishing Trade Lines:

One of the most effective ways to build a strong credit profile is by establishing trade lines with vendors and suppliers who report to credit bureaus. Look for vendors willing to extend credit terms and make timely payments to demonstrate your business's creditworthiness. Consistently meeting payment obligations and maintaining positive relationships with suppliers can help build a positive payment history and strengthen your credit profile.

6.2 Applying for Business Credit Cards:

Applying for a business credit card is another strategy for building and managing your business credit. Choose a card that offers favorable terms and rewards that align with your business needs. Use the card responsibly, making timely payments and keeping balances low relative to your credit limit, to demonstrate financial responsibility and improve your creditworthiness.

6.3 Making Timely Payments:

Making timely payments on your credit accounts is crucial for building and maintaining a strong credit profile. Set up automatic payments or reminders to ensure you pay your bills on time, every time. Late payments can negatively impact your credit score and erode trust with creditors, so prioritize timely payments to preserve your creditworthiness.

6.4 Managing Credit Utilization:

Monitoring your credit utilization ratio—the percentage of available credit you're using—is essential for managing your credit effectively. Aim to keep your credit utilization ratio below 30% to demonstrate responsible credit usage and avoid overextending your credit. Regularly review your credit card balances and credit limits to stay within your target utilization range.

6.5 Diversifying Credit Types:

Diversifying your credit types can help you build a well-rounded credit profile and demonstrate your ability to manage different types of credit responsibly. In addition to trade lines and credit cards, consider applying for other types of credit, such as business loans, lines of credit, or equipment financing. This diversification can strengthen your credit profile and improve your overall creditworthiness.

6.6 Monitoring Your Credit Report:

Regularly monitoring your business credit report from major credit bureaus allows you to stay informed about your credit standing and detect any errors or inaccuracies that may impact your creditworthiness. Review your credit report at least annually and dispute any discrepancies promptly to ensure the accuracy of your credit information.

Conclusion:

In conclusion, Chapter 6 has provided valuable insights into building strong credit profiles for your business. By establishing trade lines, applying for business credit cards, making timely payments, managing credit utilization, diversifying credit types, and monitoring your credit report, you can proactively manage your credit and position your business for long-term success and growth. As you implement these strategies, remember to prioritize financial responsibility, proactive credit management, and continuous improvement to achieve your credit-building goals.

Chapter 7: Leveraging Business Credit for Growth

Welcome to Chapter 7 of "Credit Forge: A Blueprint for Business Credit Building." In this chapter, we will explore how you can leverage your business credit to fuel growth and expansion. Building a strong credit profile opens doors to financing options and favorable terms, empowering you to invest in strategic initiatives and capitalize on growth opportunities for your business.

7.1 Accessing Financing for Expansion:

One of the primary benefits of establishing strong business credit is access to financing for expansion. With a solid credit profile, you can qualify for loans, lines of credit, and other financing options to fund initiatives such as opening new locations, launching new products or services, or investing in marketing campaigns. By leveraging financing, you can fuel growth and scale your business operations.

7.2 Negotiating Favorable Terms:

A strong credit profile gives you leverage when negotiating financing terms with lenders and creditors. With a positive credit history, you may qualify for lower interest rates, higher credit limits, and more favorable repayment terms. Negotiate with lenders to secure the best possible terms for your business, maximizing your borrowing capacity and minimizing your cost of capital.

7.3 Investing in Marketing and Advertising:

Access to financing through business credit enables you to invest in marketing and advertising initiatives to promote your products or services and attract new customers. Whether it's launching targeted advertising campaigns, sponsoring events, or investing in digital marketing strategies, leveraging financing allows you to increase brand visibility, generate leads, and drive sales growth.

7.4 Expanding Product Lines or Services:

With sufficient financing, you can expand your product lines or services to meet evolving customer needs and market demands. Invest in research and development, product design, and manufacturing capabilities to diversify your offerings and capture new market segments. By expanding your product lines or services, you can enhance your competitive advantage and stimulate revenue growth.

7.5 Investing in Technology and Innovation:

Technology plays a critical role in driving business growth and innovation. With access to financing, you can invest in upgrading your technology infrastructure, adopting new software solutions, or developing proprietary technologies to improve operational efficiency, enhance customer experiences, and stay ahead of competitors. Leveraging financing for technology investments positions your business for long-term success in a rapidly evolving marketplace.

7.6 Acquiring or Merging with Other Businesses: Access to financing through business credit can facilitate strategic acquisitions or mergers to accelerate growth and expand market reach. Whether it's acquiring a competitor, entering new geographic markets, or diversifying into complementary industries, leveraging financing allows you to pursue growth opportunities through strategic partnerships and consolidation. Evaluate potential acquisition targets or merger opportunities and structure deals that create synergies and drive value for your business.

Conclusion:

In conclusion, Chapter 7 has highlighted the importance of leveraging business credit for growth and expansion. By accessing financing, negotiating favorable terms, investing in marketing and advertising, expanding product lines or services, investing in technology and innovation, and pursuing strategic acquisitions or mergers, you can capitalize on growth opportunities and propel your business to new heights of success. As you leverage your business credit for growth, remember to prioritize strategic planning, risk management, and financial discipline to achieve sustainable growth and long-term profitability.

Chapter 8: Risk Management and Compliance

Welcome to Chapter 8 of "Credit Forge: A Blueprint for Business Credit Building." In this chapter, we will explore the importance of risk management and compliance in maintaining a healthy business credit profile. Managing risks and ensuring compliance with relevant regulations are critical aspects of responsible credit management and safeguarding your business's financial stability and reputation.

8.1 Identifying and Assessing Risks:

The first step in effective risk management is identifying and assessing potential risks to your business. This includes financial risks such as credit defaults, cash flow disruptions, and market volatility, as well as operational risks such as supply chain disruptions, regulatory compliance issues, and cybersecurity threats. Conduct a comprehensive risk assessment to identify potential threats and vulnerabilities that may impact your business's creditworthiness and operations.

8.2 Developing Risk Mitigation Strategies:

Once you've identified and assessed risks, develop risk mitigation strategies to address and minimize their impact on your business. This may involve implementing internal controls, diversifying suppliers and customers, maintaining adequate insurance coverage, and establishing contingency plans for managing emergencies or unexpected events. By proactively addressing risks, you can reduce their likelihood and severity and protect your business from financial losses and disruptions.

8.3 Monitoring Credit Performance:

Regularly monitor your business credit performance to stay informed about changes in your credit profile and detect potential warning signs of credit deterioration. Keep track of your credit scores, payment history, credit utilization, and any negative information reported on your credit report. Promptly address any issues or discrepancies and take corrective actions to maintain a positive credit profile and minimize the impact on your business's creditworthiness.

8.4 Complying with Regulatory Requirements:

Ensure compliance with relevant regulatory requirements governing credit reporting, consumer protection, data privacy, and financial transactions. Familiarize yourself with laws such as the Fair Credit Reporting Act (FCRA), the Truth in Lending Act (TILA), and the Payment Card Industry Data Security Standard (PCI DSS) to ensure your business's credit practices are following applicable regulations. Implement policies and procedures to safeguard customer data, protect against identity theft, and maintain transparency and fairness in your credit transactions.

8.5 Establishing Internal Controls:

Establish internal controls and procedures to ensure accountability, transparency, and compliance with credit policies and regulatory requirements. This may include segregating duties, conducting regular audits and reviews, maintaining accurate records, and providing training and education to employees on credit management best practices and compliance obligations. By implementing effective internal controls, you can minimize the risk of errors, fraud, and noncompliance and maintain the integrity of your business's credit operations.

8.6 Engaging Legal and Compliance Experts:

Consider engaging legal and compliance experts to provide guidance and support in navigating complex regulatory requirements and addressing legal issues related to credit management. Consult with legal counsel, compliance specialists, and industry experts to assess regulatory risks, interpret legal requirements, and develop compliance strategies tailored to your business's needs and circumstances. By partnering with knowledgeable professionals, you can ensure your business operates in accordance with the law and maintains a strong commitment to ethical and responsible credit practices.

Conclusion:

In conclusion, Chapter 8 has emphasized the importance of risk management and compliance in maintaining a healthy business credit profile. By identifying and assessing risks, developing risk mitigation strategies, monitoring credit performance, complying with regulatory requirements, establishing internal controls, and engaging legal and compliance experts, you can effectively manage risks, ensure compliance, and safeguard your business's financial stability and reputation. As you navigate the complexities of credit management and compliance, prioritize proactive risk mitigation, continuous monitoring, and a commitment to ethical and responsible business practices to achieve long-term success and sustainability.

Chapter 9: Monitoring and Maintaining Business Credit

  Welcome to Chapter 9 of "Credit Forge: A Blueprint for Business Credit Building." In this chapter, we will explore the importance of monitoring and maintaining your business credit profile. Regularly monitoring your credit performance and taking proactive steps to address any issues or discrepancies are crucial for preserving your business's creditworthiness and financial health.

9.1 Regular Credit Monitoring:

Establish a routine for monitoring your business credit reports from major credit bureaus, such as Dun & Bradstreet, Experian, and Equifax. Set up alerts or reminders to review your credit reports periodically and stay informed about any changes or updates to your credit profile. Monitoring your credit regularly allows you to detect errors, inaccuracies, or fraudulent activity promptly and take corrective actions to address them.

9.2 Reviewing Credit Scores and Factors:

Pay close attention to your business credit scores and the factors influencing them, such as payment history, credit utilization, length of credit history, and public records. Understand how changes in these factors can impact your credit scores and take proactive measures to maintain or improve your creditworthiness. Identify areas for improvement and focus on addressing any negative factors to strengthen your credit profile over time.

9.3 Disputing Errors and Inaccuracies:

If you identify any errors or inaccuracies on your business credit reports, take immediate steps to dispute them with the relevant credit bureaus. Submit a formal dispute letter outlining the inaccuracies and providing supporting documentation to substantiate your claims. Follow up with the credit bureaus to ensure your dispute is resolved promptly and accurately reflected in your credit reports.

9.4 Addressing Negative Information:

If your business credit reports contain negative information, such as late payments, defaults, or collections, take proactive steps to address these issues and mitigate their impact on your creditworthiness. Communicate with creditors to negotiate payment arrangements, settle outstanding debts, or request goodwill adjustments to remove negative information from your credit reports. By addressing negative information promptly and responsibly, you can minimize its long-term impact on your credit profile.

9.5 Managing Credit Utilization:

Keep your credit utilization ratio—the percentage of available credit you're using—within a manageable range to demonstrate responsible credit management. Aim to keep your credit utilization below 30% to maintain a positive credit profile and maximize your creditworthiness. Pay down existing balances, avoid unnecessary credit inquiries, and refrain from opening new credit accounts unnecessarily to keep your credit utilization in check.

9.6 Establishing Positive Credit Habits:

Develop positive credit habits that contribute to a strong credit profile over time. Make timely payments on your credit accounts, keep balances low relative to your credit limits, and avoid applying for multiple credit accounts simultaneously. Cultivate a culture of financial responsibility and accountability within your organization and emphasize the importance of maintaining good credit habits to preserve your business's creditworthiness.

Conclusion:

In conclusion, Chapter 9 has highlighted the importance of monitoring and maintaining your business credit profile. By regularly monitoring your credit reports, reviewing credit scores and factors, disputing errors and inaccuracies, addressing negative information, managing credit utilization, and establishing positive credit habits, you can proactively manage your business credit and ensure its long-term health and viability. As you navigate the process of monitoring and maintaining your business credit, remember to stay vigilant, proactive, and committed to preserving your business's creditworthiness and financial stability.

Congratulations! You've reached the final chapter of "Credit Forge: A Blueprint for Business Credit Building." In this chapter, we will consolidate the knowledge and strategies discussed throughout the book into a comprehensive roadmap for mastering business credit. By following this roadmap, you can navigate the complexities of credit management, build a strong credit profile, and position your business for success and growth.

10.1 Reviewing Key Concepts:

Begin by reviewing the key concepts and principles covered in the previous chapters, including the definition of business credit, its significance, building a strong credit profile, accessing financing options, risk management, compliance, and monitoring and maintaining business credit. Ensure you have a solid understanding of these concepts before proceeding further.

10.2 Setting Clear Objectives:

Define clear objectives and goals for your business credit-building journey. Determine what you hope to achieve, whether it's securing financing for expansion, improving your credit scores, or building strong relationships with creditors and suppliers. Setting clear objectives will guide your efforts and help measure your progress along the way.

10.3 Establishing a Credit Management Plan:

Develop a comprehensive credit management plan outlining the strategies and tactics you will implement to build and maintain your business credit. This plan should include steps such as obtaining a separate business identification, opening a dedicated business bank account, establishing trade lines, applying for business credit cards, and monitoring your credit performance regularly.

10.4 Implementing Best Practices:

Implement best practices for managing your business credit effectively. Make timely payments on your credit accounts, keep credit utilization low, diversify credit types, and maintain positive credit habits. Prioritize financial responsibility, proactive credit management, and transparency in your credit transactions to build trust and credibility with creditors and suppliers.

10.5 Navigating Financing Options:

Explore various financing options available to your business, such as traditional bank loans, SBA loans, business lines of credit, business credit cards, and alternative financing solutions. Evaluate each option based on factors like interest rates, repayment terms, eligibility requirements, and potential impact on your business's financial health and growth objectives.

10.6 Monitoring and Adapting:

Continuously monitor your business credit performance and adapt your credit management strategies as needed. Regularly review your credit reports, credit scores, and factors influencing your creditworthiness. Address any errors, inaccuracies, or negative information promptly and take corrective actions to maintain or improve your credit profile over time.

10.7 Seeking Professional Guidance:

Consider seeking professional guidance from financial advisors, credit counselors, legal counsel, and compliance experts to navigate complex credit issues and regulatory requirements. Leverage their expertise and insights to develop effective credit management strategies and address any challenges or obstacles you encounter along the way.

Conclusion:

In conclusion, mastering business credit requires a combination of knowledge, strategy, and diligence. By following the roadmap outlined in this chapter and throughout the book, you can build a strong credit profile, access financing options, mitigate risks, ensure compliance, and position your business for long-term success and growth. Remember to stay committed to your objectives, stay informed about changes in the credit landscape, and adapt your strategies as needed to achieve your business goals. With dedication and perseverance, you can master business credit and unlock opportunities for success in your entrepreneurial journey.

Conclusion

As we come to the end of "Credit Forge: A Blueprint for Business Credit Building," it's important to reflect on the journey we've taken together and the significance of mastering business credit. Throughout this book, we've explored the fundamentals of business credit, strategies for building and maintaining a strong credit profile, and the role of credit in driving business growth and success. Mastering business credit is not just about managing numbers and financial transactions—it's about empowering yourself with the knowledge and tools to navigate the complexities of credit effectively. By mastering business credit, you gain the ability to access financing options, negotiate favorable terms, mitigate risks, and build trust and credibility with stakeholders. However, the journey doesn't end here. Business credit is an ever-evolving landscape, influenced by economic trends, regulatory changes, and technological advancements. To stay ahead of the curve, it's essential to continue your learning and growth journey. Stay informed about changes in the credit industry, explore new financing options, and adapt your strategies to meet the evolving needs of your business. As you continue your journey, remember that success in business is not just about financial metrics—it's about making a positive impact, creating value for your customers, and building a sustainable and thriving enterprise. Armed with the knowledge and tools gained from this book, we wish you success and prosperity in your business endeavors. May you navigate the complexities of business credit with confidence and determination, and may your entrepreneurial journey be filled with growth, innovation, and fulfillment. Here's to your continued learning and growth, and to the success and prosperity that lie ahead.

ABOUT THE AUTHOR

Antwone Dixon is a seasoned business professional with over 16 years of experience in various industries. Throughout his career, Antwone has demonstrated a strong passion for entrepreneurship and business development, leveraging his expertise to help businesses thrive in competitive markets. With a deep understanding of the importance of business credit in fueling growth and success, Antwone has dedicated himself to mastering the intricacies of credit management and sharing his knowledge with others. His insights into building, managing, and leveraging business credit have empowered countless entrepreneurs and small business owners to achieve their financial goals and realize their business aspirations. Antwone's commitment to excellence and continuous learning has earned him a reputation as a trusted advisor and thought leader in the field of business credit. Through his writing and mentorship, he continues to inspire and educate individuals to navigate the complexities of business credit effectively and unlock opportunities for success in their entrepreneurial endeavors.

Notes

<u>Notes</u>

<u>Notes</u>

<u>Notes</u>

<u>Notes</u>

<u>Notes</u>

<u>Notes</u>

<u>Notes</u>

<u>Notes</u>

<u>Notes</u>

<u>Notes</u>

<u>Notes</u>

<u>Notes</u>

<u>Notes</u>

<u>Notes</u>

<u>Notes</u>

<u>Notes</u>

<u>Notes</u>

<u>Notes</u>

Notes

<u>Notes</u>

<u>Notes</u>

<u>Notes</u>

<u>Notes</u>

<u>Notes</u>

<u>Notes</u>

<u>Notes</u>

<u>Notes</u>

Notes

<u>Notes</u>

<u>Notes</u>

<u>Notes</u>

<u>Notes</u>

<u>Notes</u>

<u>Notes</u>

<u>Notes</u>

www.ingramcontent.com/pod-product-compliance
Lightning Source LLC
Chambersburg PA
CBHW070803290526
45795CB00002B/608